Kingfisher Young Knowledge

Insects

Barbara Taylor

Contents

6 What is an insect?

An insect is a small animal with six legs and three parts to its body. A hard outer skeleton covers and protects an insect's body like a suit of armour.

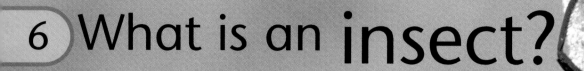

Dragonfly

On the wing

Most insects have one or two pairs of wings. Their wings are thin flaps that are made from the outer body covering. They are joined to the middle part of an insect's body, which is called the thorax.

skeleton – a structure that supports an animal's body

Early insects

The first insects lived on Earth over 400 million years ago, long before people were around. This insect was trapped in the sticky sap oozing from a tree and preserved for millions of years.

Not an insect!

Spiders, such as this house spider, are not insects. Spiders have eight legs and only two parts to their body. The head and thorax are joined together. They do not have wings either.

All kinds of insects

There are millions of different kinds of insects, which are divided into groups such as beetles, butterflies and moths, bees, wasps, flies and bugs.

Wasps

Wasps belong to a group of insects that also includes bees and ants. A wasp has a narrow 'waist' and folds its wings along the sides of its body.

bugs – insects with sucking mouthparts

Flies

A fly has only one pair of wings, yet it can fly very well. The fly group includes mosquitoes, and bluebottles like this.

Butterflies

Butterflies and moths have wings covered in tiny scales, which overlap like tiles on a roof. Butterflies, such as this swallowtail, are usually brightly coloured and fly by day.

flies – insects with only one pair of wings

Big and small insects

Most insects are small beasts – even the biggest ones could sit on your hand. Their small size means they can live in small spaces and do not need much food.

Tiny fleas

Fleas live among the fur of mammals or the feathers of birds. They have claws to cling on tight, and long legs to jump from one animal to another.

mammals – *hairy animals that feed their babies on mother's milk*

Nasty nits

Head lice thrive in the warmth of human hair, sucking blood from our skin. Female head lice glue their eggs on to the hair. These are known as nits.

Giant weta

Wetas are giant crickets that live in New Zealand. They probably grew into huge insects because there were no large mammal predators to eat them.

predators – animals that hunt and eat other animals

Insect athletes

Some insects are like human athletes. They are champion sprinters, high jumpers or weightlifters. Insects use their athletic powers to find food or mates, or just to stay alive.

Weightlifting

One of these male rhinoceros beetles has managed to lift the other right off the ground! He wins the chance to mate with the females.

mate – *to breed or reproduce*

High jump
Insects that are good at the high jump, such as this leafhopper, usually have long back legs powered by strong muscles in the thorax.

Sprinting
Long legs help insects to take big strides and sprint (move fast). The legs of this tiger beetle are much longer than its body. At any time, three of its six legs usually touch the ground.

muscles – parts of the body that produce movement

Wonder wings

Insects were the first animals to fly. Flying helps insects to find food or mates and to escape danger, but it does use up a lot of energy.

Long journeys

Monarch butterflies fly thousands of kilometres every year to escape the cold winters in Canada. These long journeys are called migration.

Wing covers

Beetles, such as this ladybird, have two pairs of wings. When a beetle lands, its hard front wings cover and protect the delicate flying wings.

flexible – able to bend without breaking

Strong wings

A network of veins in an insect's wings makes them strong and flexible. You can see the veins very clearly on this cicada's wings.

veins – narrow tubes full of blood

Clever colours

Dull colours help insects to hide from predators. Bright colours or patterns warn predators to stay away because an insect is poisonous or harmful.

Warning colours

The bright red spots on this burnet moth are a warning message, which says: 'Don't eat me, I contain deadly poison'.

Fake wasp

The wasp beetle cannot sting and is not dangerous. Predators leave it alone because they think it is a real wasp and might sting them.

Hide and seek

Many insects use camouflage to hide from predators by looking like the plants they live on. This thorn bug even has a pretend thorn on its back!

camouflage – a shape, colour or pattern that helps hide an animal

Fighting back

From sharp jaws to painful stings and chemical weapons, insects have many ways of fighting back when they are attacked by predators.

Ready, aim, fire!

Bombardier beetles spray boiling hot poisons at their enemies. The poisons are mixed up inside the beetles' bodies when danger threatens.

Horrible hiss

If these cockroaches are disturbed, they make a loud, hissing noise by pushing air out of breathing holes in their sides. This startles predators, such as spiders, giving the cockroaches time to escape.

sting – *a sharp needle on an insect's body for injecting poison*

Battling beetle

The devil's coachhorse beetle defends itself by curling its abdomen over its back like a scorpion. At the same time, the beetle gives off a nasty smell, and snaps its jaws together.

abdomen – long part of an insect's body containing its digestive system

Insect senses

An insect's senses of sight, touch, smell and hearing are vital to its survival. These senses are often much better than our own but they work in different ways.

Touch and smell

Insects use their antennae to touch and smell their surroundings. This weevil's antennae have special hairs at the tips to detect smells.

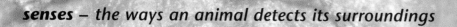

senses – the ways an animal detects its surroundings

Head fans

Scarab beetles fan out their antennae when they fly to increase their size. This helps the beetles detect any smells.

Eye spy

The big eyes of this fly are made up of thousands of very small eyes. They can see in lots of different directions at once.

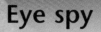

antennae – long, thin structures on an insect's head for touching and smelling

Hungry insects

Some insects, such as cockroaches, eat almost anything, but most insects feed on particular kinds of food. Their mouthparts help them to hold and chop up solid food, or suck up liquids.

Spongy mouth

Flies turn their food into a soupy mush, and then use a spongy pad (left) to mop up their meal. They can also taste their food with their feet!

mouthparts – *structures on the head used for feeding*

Jagged jaws

Insect predators need sharp, spiky jaws for holding and chopping up their prey. Insects that chew plants have blunter jaws to grind and mash up their food.

Drinking straws

Butterflies and moths feed on liquid food, such as flower nectar or rotting fruit. They suck up their food through a tube, called a proboscis, which works like a straw.

nectar – a sweet liquid made by plants

Nibbling plants

All the different parts of plants are eaten by insects. Some plant-eating insects are farmers, growing their own crops and harvesting seeds.

Leaves for lunch

Leaves do not contain much goodness so insects have to eat a lot of them. Grasshoppers are messy eaters, often tearing the leaves as they feed.

fungi – living things that cannot make their own food

Grow-your-own food

Leaf-cutter ants chew up pieces of leaves and use them to make a mushy compost. They grow fungi on the compost so they always have plenty to eat.

Wood for supper

Wood contains even less goodness than leaves, but some insects eat it. Death-watch beetle larvae spend many years eating damp wood before turning into adults like this one.

larvae – young insects that hatch out of eggs

Insect hunters

Insects hunt in three main ways. They may chase after their prey, jump out from a hiding place, or set a trap to catch a meal. Most insects hunt alone, but a few search in groups.

Look out, mantis about!

Many mantids look like leaves. They keep very still, then shoot out their long front legs to grab a passing insect. A mantis has sharp jaws to slice up its prey and scoop out the soft insides.

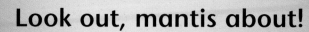

prey – an animal that is killed or eaten by another animal

Soupy snacks

Robber flies catch flying insects with their long, hairy legs. Then they turn the insides of the prey into a liquid soup and suck up their meal.

All together now

Army ants from tropical America hunt in large groups. The ants help each other to catch and kill prey. These army ants have caught a centipede.

tropical – an area near the Equator with very hot, dry weather

Life cycles

Many insects have four stages in their life cycle – egg, larva, pupa and adult. Insect groups that develop like this include beetles, butterflies, moths, flies, fleas, bees and ants.

1 Egg

A female monarch butterfly lays her eggs underneath the leaves of milkweed plants. Within a week, the eggs hatch into stripy caterpillars.

2 Larva

The hungry caterpillar eats and eats and eats. It sheds its skin several times as it grows. This is called moulting.

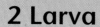

caterpillars – worm-like larvae of butterflies and moths

3 Pupa

When the caterpillar is big enough, it turns into a pupa, or chrysalis. Inside the pupa, the body of the caterpillar changes into the body of a butterfly.

4 Adult

The pupa splits open, and the adult butterfly pulls itself free. It pumps blood into its wings to stretch them out, and waits for its wings to dry. Then it flies away to look for a mate.

pupa – a protective case around a developing adult insect

Insect eggs

Almost all insects start life as eggs. The eggs are usually laid on or near food, and hidden from predators and bad weather. Very few insects look after their eggs.

Easy meals

Dung beetles shape animal dung into a ball, which they roll to a safe place. The female lays her eggs inside the dung ball so the young have food when they hatch.

hatch – come out of an egg

Caring parent

Female earwigs guard their eggs for months until they hatch. When they hatch, the babies look like their mother, but without wings.

Male on guard

This male damselfly is holding the female's neck while she lays her eggs on the stems of plants under the water. When the eggs hatch, the young live underwater for the first year.

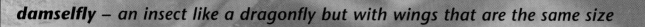

damselfly – *an insect like a dragonfly but with wings that are the same size*

Living together

Most insects live alone, but a few kinds live and work together in groups. They are called social insects. All ants and termites, and some bees and wasps are social insects.

Royal ruler
A big, fat queen termite lays all the eggs in a nest. The smaller workers carry her eggs away, and bring food for their queen.

social – *living in a group with others of the same kind, or species*

Paper nest

Paper wasps make their nest by chewing up wood and mixing it with their spit to make wasp 'paper'. Inside the nest are lots of tiny boxes, called cells, where young wasps can develop.

Special sewing

Weaver ants work together as a team to make a nest from leaves glued together with sticky silk. One ant working on its own would not be strong enough to do this.

queen – *a female that lays the eggs in a group of social insects*

34 Honeybee hive

People build artificial nests, called hives, for honeybees. The honeybees make honey from flower nectar mixed with their spit. Bee-keepers take this honey for people to eat.

Wax city

Honeybees use wax made in their bodies to build rows of six-sided boxes, called cells. These cells fit closely together to make a thin sheet called a honeycomb.

artificial – man-made

Queen bee

The big bee in the middle of this picture is a queen honeybee. She lays all the eggs in a honeybee hive.

Bee-keeper

Bee-keepers lift the honeycombs out to check on the honey and the baby bees inside. They wear special clothes to protect them from bee stings.

bee-keeper – a person who looks after honeybee hives

Friends and foes

Many insects are our friends because they help flower seeds develop, and are an important link in food chains. Some insects cause problems because they eat crops or carry diseases.

Pollen carriers

Many flowers rely on insects to carry a yellow dust, called pollen, to other flowers of the same kind. Pollen has to join with the eggs inside flowers before seeds can develop.

foes – enemies

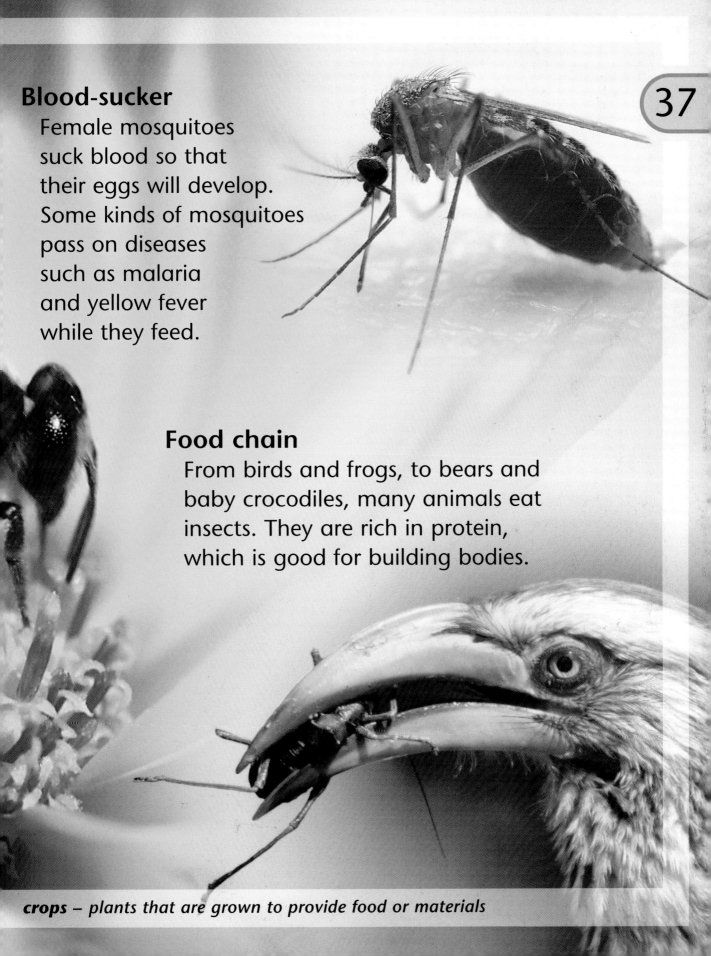

Blood-sucker

Female mosquitoes
suck blood so that
their eggs will develop.
Some kinds of mosquitoes
pass on diseases
such as malaria
and yellow fever
while they feed.

Food chain

From birds and frogs, to bears and
baby crocodiles, many animals eat
insects. They are rich in protein,
which is good for building bodies.

crops – plants that are grown to provide food or materials

Water insects

Many insects live in fresh water, where there is plenty of food and protection from predators. Some skate over the surface, some swim, while others lurk on the bottom.

Spare air

Great diving beetles collect air from the surface of the water. They store the air under their wing covers, so they can breathe while they are underwater.

fresh water – *the water in lakes, streams, ponds and puddles*

Water walker

Pond skaters can walk on the surface of the water. They have very long legs which spread their weight over a wide area so they do not sink.

Baby dragons

Baby dragonflies live under the water, but the adults live in the air. Baby dragonflies are fierce hunters and eat fish.

Night lights

Insects glow in the dark to attract a mate or prey, warn their friends of danger, or tell predators that they taste bad.

Come and get me

Fireflies and glow-worms are beetles that come out at night. Some glow all the time, while others flash their lights on and off in a particular pattern. These light signals are used to attract a mate.

glow-worms – *wingless female beetles that glow in the dark*

Cave curtains

Small flies from New Zealand shine their light down sticky strands hanging from the roof of caves. Prey insects are attracted to the glowing curtain and trapped on the strands.

Glowing bugs

A firefly produces a short burst of light when a gas, called oxygen, mixes with chemicals inside its abdomen. This works in a similar way to the glow-in-the-dark light sticks you see at Hallowe'en.

firefly – also called lightning bug – a glowing, night-time beetle

Bucket home

Bug sleepover

Make a home for the bugs that live near you. Draw pictures of the bugs that crawl inside, and write down their names.

1

You will need
- Plastic bucket
- Pen and notepad
- Stones, leaves and grass

Find a damp, shady place near your home. Turn the bucket upside down and balance it on a pile of stones, leaves and grass. Leave it overnight and see if any creatures crawl inside.

When you have finished, remember to let the animals go.

Butterfly patterns

Paint a butterfly

The patterns on one wing of a butterfly are the same as the other side. Paint your own butterfly with matching sides.

You will need
- Card
- Pencil
- Scissors
- Paint
- Paintbrush
- Pipecleaners

1

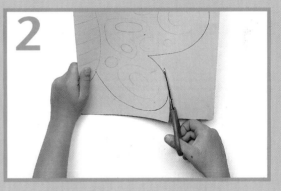

Fold the card in half, then open it out flat. Use the pencil to draw the outline of half a butterfly on one side of the fold.

2

Fold the card in half so you can still see your pencil outline. Then carefully cut out the butterfly shape.

Open the card to see the whole butterfly and use pipecleaners for its antennae.

3

Open out the card and paint one side with thick paint. Then fold your butterfly in half again and press down hard.

Model insects

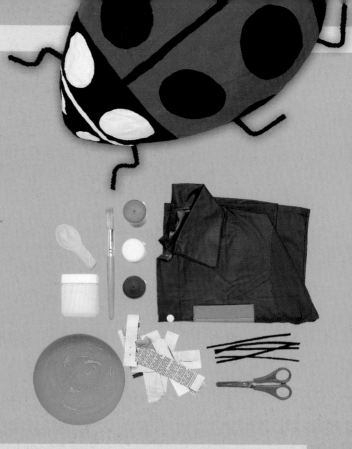

Make a ladybird

Use papier mâché to make a model of a giant ladybird. Paint the model red and black so it looks just like a real ladybird. A ladybird's bright colours warn predators that it is poisonous and tastes bad.

You will need

- Balloon
- Petroleum jelly
- Paintbrush
- Newspaper
- Wallpaper paste
- Scissors
- Paints
- Pipecleaners
- Glue or sticky tape

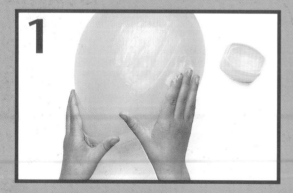

Ask an adult to help you blow up a balloon. Spread a thick layer of petroleum jelly all over the balloon, then wash your hands.

Cover the whole balloon with strips of newspaper. Brush wallpaper paste over the paper and repeat about five times.

3

Put the balloon in a warm place to dry. When the surface is hard, use the scissors to carefully cut the balloon in half.

4

Paint the balloon with ladybird colours. Use pipecleaners to make the legs, and attach them with glue or sticky tape.

Look in books to see if there are any different coloured ladybirds and paint the other papier mâché shape in those colours.

Bug mobile

Make a mobile

Hang this colourful mobile near a window, or even outside, and watch the bugs fly around the flower as the breeze blows.

Ladybird

You will need
- Coloured card
- Pencil
- Scissors
- Paintbrush
- Paints
- Thin wire
- String
- Tracing paper
- Strong thread
- Apron

Draw a large flower shape on coloured card and cut around the edge. Paint the flower with colours that you like.

Ask an adult to help you make a circle of wire. Tie four long pieces of string to the wire and knot the ends so the mobile can hang.

3

Trace or copy the bugs on these pages or draw your own on to card. Cut them out and paint them to look like bugs.

4

Ask an adult to make small holes in your flower and bugs so you can tie them to the wire circle. Your mobile is now ready to hang.

Bee

Shield bug

Dragonfly

Index